D1115041

BEST
LAWYER
JOKES EVER

BEST
LAWYER
JOKES EVER

BARNES
&NOBLE
BOOKS
NEW YORK

Copyright © 2002 by MetroBooks

ISBN 0-7607-2887-9

Book Design: Kevin McGuinness

Manufactured in the United States of America

2 4 6 8 10 7 5 3 1

HOW MANY LAWYER JOKES ARE THERE?
Only three. The rest are true stories.

Randy walked into a post office one day to see a middle-aged, balding man standing at the counter methodically placing "Love" stamps on bright pink envelopes with hearts all over them. He then took out a perfume bottle and started spraying scent all over each envelope. Randy's curiosity getting the better of her, she went up to the man and asked him what he was doing.

The man said, "I'm sending out one thousand Valentines cards signed 'Guess who?'"

"But why?" Randy asked.

"I'm a divorce lawyer," the man replied.

JACKSON, A SUCCESSFUL ATTORNEY, WAS speeding down a dark country road late one evening when he collided with a car coming from the opposite direction.

Neither driver was hurt, but Jackson, seeing that the other driver was a little shaken up, helped him from the car and offered him a drink from his hip flask. The other driver gratefully accepted, took a long swig, and handed the flask back to Jackson. He closed it and put it away.

"Aren't you going to have a drink yourself?" asked the driver.

"Sure," replied Jackson. "After the police leave."

Lauren and Maureen embarked on a transcontinental balloon voyage. Their craft was engulfed in fog, their compass gone awry. They drifted for days, completely lost and afraid of landing in the ocean. Suddenly, the clouds parted to show a sunlit meadow below. As they descended, the passengers saw a man walking his dog.

Lauren yelled to the figure below, "Where are we?"

The man yelled back, "About a half mile from town."

Once again, the balloonists became engulfed

in the mist. Lauren turned to Maureen. "He must have been a lawyer."

"A lawyer! How do you know that?"

Lauren smiled. "That's easy. The information he gave us was accurate, concise, and entirely useless."

A SENIOR PARTNER WAS INTERVIEWING a young attorney, fresh out of law school. As they reached the end of the interview, the partner asked, "What starting salary were you looking for?"

The new attorney replied, "In the neighborhood of $125,000 a year, depending on the benefits package."

"Well then," the senior partner said, "what would you say to a package of five weeks vacation, fourteen paid holidays, full medical and dental, company matching retirement fund to 50 percent of salary, and a company car leased every two years—say, a red Corvette?"

The eager young attorney sat up straight in his chair and said, "Wow! Are you kidding?"

"Yeah, but you started it."

To me, a lawyer is basically the person who knows the rules of the country. We're all throwing the dice, playing the game, moving our pieces around the board, but if there is a problem the lawyer is the only person who has read the inside of the top of the box.

—Jerry Seinfeld

THREE LAWYERS AND THREE ACCOUNTANTS got on the train in New York to go to a convention in Washington D.C. The three accountants bought one ticket each, but the three lawyers bought only one ticket between the three. When the accountants commented on the illegality of their action, the lawyers just replied, "Trust us—we're lawyers."

When the conductor entered the end of the car to collect the tickets, the three lawyers got up and all went into the bathroom together. When the conductor knocked on the bathroom door, a hand shot out with the one ticket, which the conductor duly cancelled.

On returning to their seats the three accountants expressed admiration for such a clever trick. "Well," the lawyers said modestly, "we *are* lawyers."

After the convention, all six entered Union Station for the return trip home to New York. This time the accountants bought one ticket between them, while the lawyers did not buy any tickets at all. The accountants were amazed. "Trust us," the three said. "We're lawyers."

When the conductor arrived, the three accountants quickly jumped up and went into the bathroom. As soon as the door closed, the three lawyers got up and headed for the adjoining bathroom. As the last lawyer went by the accountant's bathroom, he knocked on the door. A hand shot out with the ticket, which the lawyer quickly grabbed before entering the other bathroom.

When a person assists a criminal in breaking the law *before* the criminal gets arrested, we call him an accomplice.

When a person assists a criminal in breaking the law *after* the criminal has been arrested, we call him a defense attorney.

OUT OF CURIOSITY, AN ACCIDENT VICTIM and his lawyer attended a revival meeting being conducted by a travelling evangelist preacher, who had acquired a large following and an excellent reputation.

Much to their surprise, they discovered that the evangelist truly had the power to heal. He laid his hand on a blind man. The man jumped up and shouted, "I can see! I can see! Bless you, Father, bless you!"

Then the preacher touched a deaf man and said, "Tell me your name." The man jumped up and shouted, "I can hear! I can hear!"

Seeing the accident victim in a wheelchair, with multiple casts and bandages, the minister approached.

Suddenly, the lawyer jumped up. "Don't you *dare* touch him! The trial isn't until next week!"

A Russian, a Cuban, an American, and a lawyer were on a train. The Russian took a bottle of the best vodka out of his pack, poured some into a glass, drank it, and said, "In USSR, we have the best vodka in the world. Nowhere in the world can you find vodka as good as the one we produce in Ukraine. And we have so much of it, that we can just throw it away." With that, he opened the window and tossed out the rest of the bottle. All the others were quite impressed.

The Cuban brought out a pack of Havanas, took one cigar out of the box, lit it, and began to smoke, saying, "In Cuba, we have the best cigars in the world: Havana's. Nowhere in the world there is so many and so good cigar and we have so much of them that we can just throw them away." With that, he threw the pack of Havana's through the window. Again, everyone was quite impressed.

With that, the American stood up, opened the window, and threw out the lawyer.

MY DADDY IS A MOVIE ACTOR, AND sometimes he plays the good guy, and sometimes he plays the lawyer.

—Malcolm Ford, to his preschool classmates on what his father, actor Harrison Ford, does for a living.

A sailor took the witness stand in a trial. "Would you please tell the court," began the attorney, "if you recognize either the defendant or the plaintiff."

"Beg pardon, sir," said the sailor, "but I don't know what those terms mean."

The lawyer's eyes narrowed. "Shame on you! How can you come to testify at an important trial and not even know those basic terms?"

"Sorry, sir."

The lawyer sighed. "Okay, where were you when the accused is said to have struck the victim?"

"Sir, I was abaft the binnacle," replied the sailor.

"What? Where?" demanded the lawyer.

"Shame on you!" said the sailor. "How can you try a case about a boat and not even know those basic terms?"

A TRUCK DRIVER USED TO AMUSE HIMSELF on long trips by running over lawyers walking down the side of the road. He'd see a lawyer, swerve to the side to hit him, and hear a loud "thump."

One day, as the truck driver was driving along he saw a priest hitchhiking. He thought he'd do a good turn and offer the priest a lift. Pulling the truck over to the side of the road, he called out the window, "Where are you going, Father?"

"I'm going to a church five miles down the road," replied the priest.

"No problem, Father! I'll give you a lift. Hop on in."

With that, the happy priest climbed into the passenger seat, and the truck driver continued on.

Suddenly, the truck driver saw a lawyer walking down the road, and instinctively swerved to hit him. But then he remembered the priest sitting beside him. So at the last minute he swerved back to the road, just narrowly missing the lawyer. Although he was certain he missed the lawyer, he heard a loud "thump."

The truck driver glanced in his mirrors. Not

being able to discern where the noise was from, he turned to the priest and said, "I'm sorry, Father. I almost hit that lawyer."

"That's okay," said the priest. "I got him with the door."

Barbara went into a pet shop to buy a parrot. The shop owner pointed to three identical-looking parrots on a perch and said, "The parrot on the left costs $500."

"Wow! Why does that parrot cost so much?" asked Barbara.

"He knows how to do legal research," the owner replied.

Barbara then inquired about the next parrot. "That one costs $1,000," the owner said.

"$1,000?" Barbara asked incredulously.

"Well, he can do everything the other parrot can do, plus he knows how to write a brief that will win any case."

Astonished, Barbara inquired about the third bird.

The owner scratched his head. "To be honest, I've never seen him do a darn thing, but the other two call him Senior Partner."

A HOUSEWIFE, AN ACCOUNTANT, AND A lawyer were asked, "How much is two plus two?"

The housewife replied, "Four."

The accountant said, "I think it's either three or four. Let me run those figures through my spreadsheet one more time."

The lawyer pulled the drapes, dimmed the lights, and asked in a hushed voice, "How much do you want it to be?"

While walking down the street, Karen, a highly successful partner in a law firm, was tragically hit by a bus and killed. Her soul arrived up in heaven where she was met at the Pearly Gates by St. Peter himself.

"Welcome to heaven," said St. Peter. "I should let you know before you get settled in, though, that you are our first lawyer. Since we're not quite sure what to do with you, we're going to let you spend a day in heaven and a day in hell, and then you can choose where you would rather spend an eternity." Before Karen could protest, St. Peter pushed her in an elevator that slowly descended to the depths of hell.

Much to her surprise, when the doors

opened Karen found herself stepping out onto the putting green of a beautiful golf course. In the distance was a country club, and standing in front of her were all her old friends, including lawyers she had worked with before they passed away. They all ran up, greeted her warmly, and started to talk of old times.

After a round of golf, they went to the country club where Karen enjoyed a steak and lobster dinner. She met the devil, who was actually a nice guy, and had a great time telling jokes and dancing to the live band. Before she knew it, her day was over and it was time to return to heaven. Everybody shook Karen's hand and waved good-bye as she got back on the elevator.

The elevator slowly rose and eventually opened back up at the Pearly Gates. Karen spent her day in heaven lounging around on clouds, playing the harp, and singing with the choirs of angels. It was all very soothing and peaceful, and before she knew it, another twenty-four hours were up and it was time to make a decision.

St. Peter retrieved Karen off a cloud. "So,

you've spent your day in hell and your day in heaven. Now you must choose your eternity."

Karen paused for a moment and thought it over. "Well, I never thought I'd say this—I mean, heaven has been great and all—but, I think I had a better time in hell."

With that, St. Peter escorted Karen back to the elevator and again she descended to hell. When the doors of the elevator opened, she found herself standing in a desolate wasteland covered in filth. Her friends were burning in towers of flame as demons prodded them with pitchforks. The devil came up to her and welcomed her back.

"I don't understand," Karen stammered. "I was here only yesterday, and there was a golf course and a country club and lobster and we all danced and had a great time. Now all I see is fire and brimstone and a wasteland of filth. All my old friends are suffering. What kind of joke is this?"

The devil looked at her and smiled. "Yesterday we were recruiting you. Today, you're an associate."

WHAT DO YOU GET WHEN YOU CROSS THE Godfather with a lawyer?

An offer you can't understand.

Did you hear that the post office had to recall its series of stamps depicting famous lawyers?

People were confused about which side to spit on.

WHILE WAITING AT A RED LIGHT, MARY'S car was struck from behind. A policeman witnessed the accident and ran up to the car. "Miss, are you seriously injured?"

"How should I know?" Mary replied. "I'm a doctor, not a lawyer!"

A dying man gathered his lawyer, doctor, and his clergyman at his bedside and handed each of them an envelope containing $25,000 in cash. He made them each promise that after his death they would place the three envelopes in his coffin so he would have enough money to enjoy the afterlife.

A week later the man died. At the wake, the lawyer, doctor, and clergyman each dutifully concealed an envelope in the coffin and bid their old client and friend farewell.

By chance, these three met several months later. Soon the clergyman, feeling guilty, blurted out a confession saying that there was only $10,000 in the envelope he placed in the coffin. Rather than waste all the money, he wanted to send it to a mission in South Africa. He asked for their forgiveness.

The doctor, moved by the gentle clergyman's sincerity, confessed that he, too, had kept some of the money for a worthy medical charity. The envelope, he admitted, had only $8,000 in it. He said that he could not bring himself to waste the money so frivolously when it could be used to benefit others.

By this time the lawyer was seething with self-righteous outrage. He expressed his deep disappointment in the felonious behavior of his two oldest and most trusted friends. "I am the only one who kept his promise to our dying friend. I want you both to know that the envelope that I placed in the coffin contained the full amount. Indeed, my envelope contained my personal check for the entire $25,000."

A CLIENT, ANGRY AT HIS OUTRAGEOUS legal bill, asked his lawyer to itemize costs. The statement he received included this item:

"Was walking down the street and saw you on the other side. Walked to the corner to cross at the light, crossed the street, and walked quickly to catch up with you. Got close and saw it wasn't you—$50.00."

Miss Simberlund, a sixth-grade teacher, posed the following problem to one of her classes: "A wealthy man dies and leaves $10 million. One-fifth is to go to his wife, one-fifth is to go to his son, one-sixth to his butler, and the rest to charity. Now, what does each get?"

After a very long silence in the classroom, Little Johnny raised his hand. Miss Simberlund called on him for his answer.

With complete sincerity in his voice, he called out, "A lawyer!"

GOD SAVE US FROM A LAWYER'S ETCETERA.
—French proverb

A man sat down at a bar, looked into his shirt pocket, and ordered a double scotch.

A few minutes later, the man again peeked into his pocket and ordered another double. This routine continued for some time, until finally, after once more looking into his pocket, the man told the bartender that he'd had enough.

"I've got to ask you," the bartender said, "what's with the pocket business?"

"Oh," said the man, "I have my lawyer's picture in here. When he starts to look honest, I know I've had enough."

NEWMARK WAS STUCK IN A TRAFFIC JAM that hadn't moved for more than half an hour. Looking out his car window he saw a kid on a skateboard weaving his way towards him through the line of stranded vehicles.

"Hey kid, what's the hold-up?" he asked.

"It's some crazy lawyer," replied the kid. "He's lying in the middle of the road and he's doused himself with petrol. He's threatening to set fire to himself. We're taking up a collection for him. Would you like to donate, mister?"

"How much have you got so far?" Newmark inquired.

"Oh," said the kid, "about thirty boxes of matches and twenty-three lighters."

Ralph was forced to take a day off from work to appear for a minor traffic summons. He grew increasingly restless as he waited hour after endless hour for his case to be heard.

When his name was called late in the afternoon, he stood before the judge only to hear that court would be adjourned for the rest of the afternoon and he would have to return the next day.

"What for?" Ralph snapped at the judge.

His Honor, equally irked by a tedious day and

sharp query, roared in response, "Twenty dollars contempt of court. That's why!" Then, just as Ralph was checking his wallet, the judge sighed. "That's all right. You don't have to pay now."

"I wasn't," Ralph replied. "I was just seeing if I had enough for two more words."

HAVING RECENTLY PASSED ON, THE lawyer found himself in hell. He accompanied the devil to a room filled with nothing but clocks. Each clock turned at a different speed and was labeled with the name of a different occupation.

The lawyer turned to the devil and asked, "Why does each clock move at a different speed?"

"Each clock is set to turn at the rate that occupation sins on Earth," the devil replied.

The lawyer frowned. "I can't seem to find my occupation. Where is the lawyers' clock?"

Puzzled, the devil scanned the room. "Oh, that's right! We keep that clock in the workshop and use it as a fan."

What's the difference between a dry cleaner and a lawyer? The cleaner pays if he loses your suit. If a lawyer loses your suit, he'll take you to the cleaners.

A GOLFER HOOKED HIS TEE SHOT OVER A hill and onto the next fairway. Walking towards his ball, he came upon another golfer lying on the ground and groaning in pain.

"I'm an attorney," the wincing golfer said, "and this is going to cost you $5,000!"

"I'm sorry, I'm really sorry," the first golfer replied. "But I did yell 'fore.'"

The attorney stood up and brushed himself off. "I'll take it."

A gang of thieves broke into a lawyer's club by mistake. The old legal beagles gave them a fight for their lives—and their money. The gang was very happy to escape.

"It ain't so bad, Louie," one crook noted when

the gang got back to their hideout. "We got out with $25 between us."

"I warned you to stay clear of lawyers!" the boss screamed. "We had over $100 when we broke in dat joint!"

A DEFENSE ATTORNEY WAS CROSS-examining a police officer during a felony trial:

Q: Officer, did you see my client fleeing the scene?

A: No sir, but I subsequently observed a person matching the description of the offender running several blocks away.

Q: Officer, who provided this description?

A: The officer who responded to the scene.

Q: A fellow officer provided the description of this so-called offender. Do you trust your fellow officers?

A: Yes, sir, with my life.

Q: With your life? Let me ask you this, then, Officer—do you have a locker room in the po-lice station, a room where you change your clothes in preparation for your daily duties?

A: Yes, sir, we do.

Q: And do you have a locker in that room?
A: Yes, sir, I do.
Q: And do you have a lock on your locker?
A: Yes, sir.
Q: Now why is it, Officer, if you trust your fellow officers with your life, that you find it necessary to lock your locker in a room that you share with those same officers?
A: You see, sir, we share the building with a court complex, and sometimes lawyers have been known to walk through that room.

Two lawyers were walking through the courthouse, negotiating a case.
"Look," the first lawyer said to the other, "let's be honest with each other."
"Okay, you first," replied the second.
And that was the end of the discussion.

THE JUDICIAL PROCESS IS LIKE A COW. The public is impaled on its horns, the government has it by the tail, and all the while the lawyers are milking it.

A preacher and an attorney were talking one day about the mistakes they made in their respective professions and how they dealt with them. The lawyer boasted that, because he was a lawyer, if he made a really big mistake he just shuffled a few papers, pulled a few legal maneuvers and covered it all up. If it was a small mistake, he just ignored it and went on with life.

The attorney turned to the preacher and asked, "How do you do it, Preacher?"

The preacher said, "Well, if it is a really *large* mistake, I turn to the Lord and ask for forgiveness."

The attorney interrupted him and asked, "But what about small mistakes? How do you handle them?"

The preacher replied, "Well, here's an example. Just last Sunday, in my sermon, I was quoting Jesus from the gospel of John, chapter eight, where he said, 'You are of your father the devil, he was a liar from the beginning.' Instead I said, 'You are of your father the devil, he was *lawyer* from the beginning.'"

Upon hearing this, the lawyer became indignant. He retorted, "Well, how did you handle that one?"

The preacher replied, "It was such a small mistake that I just ignored it and went on."

A LOCAL NEWSPAPER MISTAKENLY PRINTED an obituary for the town's oldest practicing lawyer. He called them immediately and threatened to sue unless they printed a retraction.

The next day, the following notice appeared: "We regret that the report of Attorney Smith's death was in error."

It seems that a lawyer had a little too much to drink one night, and on his way home rear-ended a car in front of him.

The lawyer got out of his car, walked over to the driver of the other car, and sneered, "Boy, are you in trouble. I'm a lawyer!"

The driver looked at him out his window and replied, "No, you're in trouble. I'm a judge."

The Lawyer's Motto

"INSOFAR AS MANIFESTATIONS OF functional deficiencies are agreed by any and all concerned parties to be imperceivable, and are so stipulated, it is incumbent upon said heretofore mentioned parties to exercise the deferment of otherwise pertinent maintenance procedures."

In other words, if it ain't broke, don't fix it.

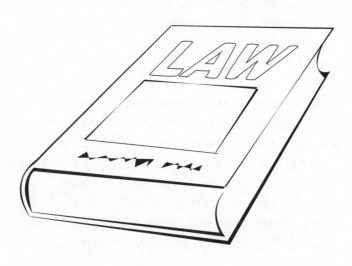

Rita, an investment counselor, decided to go out on her own. She was shrewd and diligent, so business kept coming in. Pretty soon Rita realized that she needed an in-house counsel, and she began to interview new lawyers.

"As I'm sure you understand," she started off with one of the first applicants, "in a business like this our personal integrity must be beyond question." She leaned forward. "Mr. Peterson, are you an honest lawyer?"

"Honest?" replied the job prospect. "Let me tell you something about honest. Why, I'm so honest that my father lent me $15,000 for my education and I paid back every penny the minute I tried my very first case."

"Impressive. And what sort of case was that?"

The lawyer squirmed in his seat. "He sued me for the money."

AFTER HAVING RECENTLY GONE THROUGH a divorce and experiencing many other legal problems, Larry had become thoroughly disgusted with lawyers. One evening in a bar, the conversation got around to his pet peeve and he started to complain.

"All lawyers are jerks," he loudly proclaimed.

Another man nearby heard the insult, looked disturbed, and sauntered over to Larry. "Look, I heard what you said," he sneered. "I am highly offended by it."

"Why is that?" Larry retorted. "Are you a lawyer?"

"No! I'm not a *lawyer*," the other man replied. "I'm a jerk."

LAWYER: AN INDIVIDUAL WHOSE PRIN-
ciple role is to protect his clients from others of his profession.

—Anonymous

When Oklahoma was first settled, the growing population supported a small community of lawyers. One lawyer became quite successful through handling disputes between ranchers and farmers. He made so much money, in fact, that he was able to send his son away to college.

After graduating, his son returned to Oklahoma seeking work in his father's office in the hopes of learning the law. The lawyer welcomed his son into the firm and gave him a job as a clerk. On his son's first day, a rancher, deeply tanned from years of toil under the Oklahoma sun, called on the lawyer. His hands were rough and callused, and he was dressed for the range.

"I'm a ranch hand at the Smith ranch," the rancher said, "and I have worked there since I was very young. For all these years I have tended to all the animals on the ranch, including a small herd of cows. I raised the cows, fed them, and cared for them. It has always been my understanding that I was the owner of the cows. Mr. Smith died recently, and his son has inherited the ranch. His son believes, as the cows were raised on his family's land and were fed by his family's hay, that they are his cows. I need you to help me."

The lawyer smiled and put his hand on the rancher's shoulder. "I have heard enough, and

I will take your case. Don't worry about the cows."

After expressing extreme gratitude, the rancher left the lawyer's office.

A short time later, the next client arrived. He was young and well-groomed, and appeared quite wealthy. "My name is Smith," he explained to the lawyer, "and I own a ranch near here. For many years one of my ranch hands has taken care of my family's herds, including some cows. The cows were raised on our land and fed with our hay. They are obviously my cows. Yet the hand believes, as he raised them and cared for them, that they are his. I would like to resolve the matter of the ownership of the cows."

The lawyer smiled and replied, "I have heard enough. I will take your case. Don't worry about the cows."

After Smith left the office, the lawyer's son came over to his father, looking puzzled. "I don't understand," he said. "I may not know much about the law, but it seems to me that there is a serious problem with these cows and you just told both sides not to worry."

Chuckling, the lawyer explained, "I told them not to worry about the *cows,* son, and they shouldn't. The cows will be ours."

Overheard: A conversation between two small boys, not yet old enough to be in school.

"My name is Billy. What's yours?" asked the first boy.

"Tommy," replied the second.

"My daddy's an accountant," said Billy. "What does your daddy do for a living?"

"My daddy's a lawyer," Tommy answered.

"Honest?" asked Billy.

"No, just the regular kind."

IMAGINE THE APPEALS, DISSENTS, AND remandments if lawyers had written the Ten Commandments.

—Harry Bender

A lawyer was in a meeting with his recently divorced client. "Mr. Smedley, I have some good news and I have some bad news."

Mr. Smedley replied, "I could really use some good news. What is it?"

"Your ex-wife is not making you pay on any inheritance you receive."

"Well, that's great to hear!" replied Mr. Smedley. "All right, now what about the bad news?"

"She's marrying your father."

NICHOLS, A HIGH-PRICED ATTORNEY, HAD a summer home in the backwoods section of Maine, where he retreated for several weeks each year. Every summer, he would invite a friend to spend a week or two with him. Most recently, Nichols had invited his Czechoslovakian buddy, who, eager to get a freebee out of a lawyer, agreed to come along.

They had a splendid time in the country, rising early and living in the great outdoors. Early one morning, Nichols and his Czechoslovakian companion went out to pick berries for their morning breakfast. As they went around the berry patch, gathering blueberries and rasp- berries in tremendous quantities, along came two huge bears, one male and the other female. Nichols, seeing the two bears, immedi- ately dashed for cover. His friend wasn't so lucky, though, and the male bear reached him and swallowed him whole. Nichols ran back to his Mercedes, tore into town as fast as he could, and got the local backwoods sheriff. The sheriff grabbed his shotgun and dashed back to the berry patch with the lawyer.

Luckily, the two bears were still there. "He's in *that* one!" cried Nichols, pointing to the male, while visions of lawsuits from his friend's family danced in his head. The sheriff looked at the bears, and without batting an eye, leveled his gun, took careful aim, and shot the female bear.

"Whatddya do that for?" screamed Nichols. "I told you he's in the other bear!"

"Exactly," replied the sheriff. "Would *you* believe a lawyer who told you that the Czech was in the male?"

Y ou are lying so clumsily," said the judge to the defendant, "that I would advise you to get a lawyer."

WHEN LAWYERS DIE, WHY ARE THEY buried in a hole twenty-four feet in the ground?

Because deep down, they are all really nice guys!

ow can I ever thank you," gushed a woman to Clarence Darrow after he had solved her legal troubles.

"My dear woman," Darrow replied, "ever since the Phoenicians invented money there has been only one answer to that question."

A LAWYER NAMED STRANGE LIKED TO plan ahead. One afternoon, he went shopping for his tombstone. After he made his selection, the stonecutter asked Strange what he wanted the inscription to read.

"'Here lies Strange, an honest man and a lawyer,'" responded Strange.

"Sorry, but I can't do that," replied the stonecutter. "In this state, it's against the law to bury two people in the same grave. However, I could put 'Here lies an honest lawyer.'"

"But no one will know who it is," protested Strange.

"Certainly will," retorted the stonecutter. "People will read it and exclaim, 'That's strange!'"

The defendant, on trial for assault and battery, claimed he barely pushed the victim. The prosecuting attorney, treating this story with derision, was aggressively cross-examining the defendant.

The prosecutor finally invited the defendant to step down from the witness stand and use him to demonstrate exactly how hard he had pushed the victim. Secretly the prosecutor assumed that, reacting to the hostility of the cross-examination, the accused would push him fairly hard and thereby guarantee his conviction.

The defendant had barely stepped off the witness stand when he started punching and battering the prosecutor. After he had given him a righteous thrashing, he turned to the jury. "I pushed the victim in this case about one-twentieth as hard."

The jury unanimously acquitted him.

SOMEONE MISTAKENLY LEFT THE CAGES open in the reptile house at the zoo and there were snakes slithering all over the place.

Frantically, the keeper tried everything, but he couldn't get the slippery animals back into their cages. Finally he yelled, "Quick, call a lawyer!"

"A lawyer? Why?"

"We need someone who speaks their language!"

A tourist wandered into a back alley in San Francisco's Chinatown and came across an antique shop. Picking through the objects on display, he discovered a detailed, life-sized bronze sculpture of a rat. The sculpture was so detailed and unique that he picked it up and asked the shop owner what it cost.

"Twelve dollars for the rat, sir," replied the shop owner, "and $1,000 more for the story behind it."

"You can keep the story, old man," the tourist said, "but I'll take the rat."

With the transaction complete, the tourist left the store with the bronze rat under his arm. As he crossed the street in front of the store, two live rats emerged from a sewer drain and fell into step behind him. Nervously looking over his shoulder, he began to walk faster, but every time he passed another sewer drain, more rats came out and joined the procession. By the time he walked two blocks, at least a hundred rats were at his heels and people began to point and shout. The tourist walked even faster, and soon broke into a trot as multitudes of rats swarmed from sewers, basements, vacant lots, and abandoned cars. Rats by the thousands were at his heels when he spotted the waterfront at the bottom of the hill. He panicked and began to run at full speed.

No matter how fast he ran the rats kept up, squealing hideously. Now there weren't just thousands, but millions, so that by the time he came rushing up to the water's edge, a trail of rats twelve city blocks long was behind him. Making a mighty leap, the tourist jumped up onto a light post, grasping it with one arm while he hurled the bronze rat, as far as he could heave it, into the San Francisco Bay with the other arm. Pulling up his legs and clinging to the light post, the man watched in amazement as the seething tide of rats surged over the breakwater into the sea, where they drowned.

Shaken and mumbling, the bewildered tourist made his way back to the antique shop.

"Ah," said the owner, with a smile, as he spotted the tourist. "I see you've come back for the rest of the story."

"No," replied the tourist. "I was wondering if you had a bronze lawyer."

TWO DIVORCE LAWYERS WERE HAVING drinks in a lounge after a grueling day in the courts. In walked the most stunning woman either of the lawyers had seen in a long time.

One of the lawyers remarked, "Boy! I sure would like to screw her!"

"Out of what?" the other replied.

A big-city lawyer was representing the railroad in a lawsuit filed by an old rancher. The rancher's prize bull was missing from the section through which the railroad passed, and the rancher only wanted to be paid the fair value of the bull. The case was scheduled to be tried before the justice of the peace in the back room of the general store.

The attorney for the railroad immediately cornered the rancher and tried to convince him to settle out of court. The lawyer did his best selling job, and finally the rancher agreed to take half of what he was originally asking for.

After the rancher had signed the release and took the check, the young lawyer couldn't resist gloating a little over his success. He told the rancher, "You know, I hate to tell you this, old man, but I put one over on you in there. I couldn't have won the case. The engineer was asleep and the fireman was in the caboose when the train went through your ranch that morning. I didn't have one witness to put on the stand. I bluffed you!"

The old rancher replied, "Well, I'll tell you, young feller, I was a little worried about win-

ning that case myself. That durned bull came
home this morning."

THREE PROUD MOTHERS WERE DESCRIBING
the virtues of their children. The first said,
"My daughter, the surgeon, has invented a new
artificial liver that has saved the lives of
countless patients."
   The second proudly exclaimed, "My son, the
physicist, has developed a new energy source
capable of heating thousands of homes with
absolutely no pollution."
   "That's nothing," replied the third mother.
"My son, the lawyer, has discovered a new ac-
counting system that allows him to bill clients
for the time he spends on the golf course!"

Lawyers and computers have been pro-
liferating since 1970.
   Unfortunately, lawyers, unlike computers, have not gotten twice as smart and half
as expensive every eighteen months.

DEWEY CHEATHAM AND HOWE LAW FIRM

PLEASE CHECK ONLY ONE

☐ **AWARDED DAMAGES**......... **$20,000**

☐ **ACQUITTAL**..................... **$15,000**

☐ **CASE THROWN-OUT**.......... **$10,000**

☐ **HUNG JURY**.............. **$5,000**

A PRIEST WAS CALLED TO THE HOUSE
of an elderly attorney.

"How is the patient?" he asked the doctor.

"I'm afraid he's lying at death's door."

The priest sighed. "Poor soul. Going to meet
his maker, and he's still lying."

The receptionist for a law firm answered
the phone the morning after the firm's
senior partner had unexpectedly
passed away. "Is Mr. Spencer there?" asked
the client on the phone.

"I'm very sorry, but Mr. Spencer passed
away last night," the receptionist replied. "Can
I have anyone else help you?" The client said
no and hung up.

Ten minutes later, the same client called
again and asked for Mr. Spencer, his ex-wife's
attorney.

"You just called a few minutes ago, didn't

you?" the receptionist said. "Mr. Spencer has died. I'm not making this up."

Fifteen minutes later, the client called for the third time, still asking for Mr. Spencer. The receptionist was irked. "I've told you *twice* already. Mr. Spencer is dead. He is not here! Why do you keep asking for him? Don't you understand what I'm saying?"

"I understand you perfectly," the client replied. "I just like to hear you say it."

A MAN WALKING ALONG A BEACH CAME across an odd-looking bottle. Not being one to ignore tradition, he rubbed it and, much to his surprise, out popped a genie.

"For releasing me from the bottle, I will grant you three wishes," began the genie. "But there's a catch. For each of your wishes, every lawyer in the world will receive double of what you asked for."

First the man wished for a Ferrari. Poof! A beautiful red Ferrari appeared in front of him. "Now, remember, every lawyer in the world has just been given two Ferraris," said the genie. "What's your next wish?"

"I could really use $1 million," replied the man, and poof! One million dollars appeared at his feet.

"Now every lawyer in the world is $2 million richer," reminded the genie. "What's your third wish?"

The man thought for a minute and smiled. "Well, I've always wanted to donate a kidney."

Two partners from a law firm were having lunch when one suddenly jumped up from the table. "I have to go back to the office," he cried. "I forgot to lock the safe!"

"What are you worried about?" asked the other. "We're both here."

A PRIEST, A DOCTOR, AND A LAWYER WERE waiting one morning for a particularly slow group of golfers.

"What's with these guys?" snapped the

lawyer. "We've been waiting for fifteen minutes!"

"I don't know," the doctor sneered, "but I've never seen such ineptitude."

"Hey, here comes the groundskeeper. Let's have a word with him. Say, George," the priest called. "What's with that group ahead of us? They're rather slow, aren't they?"

George smiled at the group. "Oh, yes, that's a group of blind firefighters. They lost their sight last year saving our clubhouse from a fire, so we let them play for free anytime."

The group was silent for a moment.

"That's so sad," the priest quietly said. "I think I'll say a special prayer for them tonight."

"Good idea," the doctor said, shamefully. "And I'm going to contact my ophthalmologist buddy to see if there's anything he can do for them."

The lawyer looked at the groundskeeper. "Why can't these guys play at night?"

HELL HATH NO FURY LIKE THE LAWYER
of a woman scorned.

A lawyer was walking down the street
when he saw an auto accident. He
rushed over and started handing out
business cards.

"I saw the whole thing," he said. "I'll take
either side."

A SNAKE AND A RABBIT WERE RACING
along a pair of intersecting forest pathways
when they collided, and they began to argue
with one another as to who was at fault for
the mishap. When the snake remarked that
he had been blind since birth, and thus
should be given additional leeway, the rabbit
said that he, too, was blind. The two animals
then forgot about the collision and began
commiserating about the problems with
being blind.

The snake said that his greatest sadness

was the loss of his identity. He had never been able to see his reflection in water, and for that reason did not know exactly what he looked like. He didn't even know what kind of animal he was.

The rabbit felt the same pain. Seeing a way that they could help each other, the rabbit proposed that one feel the other from head to toe, then try to describe what the other animal was. The snake agreed, and began by winding himself around the rabbit.

After a few moments he announced, "You have very soft, fuzzy fur, long ears, big rear feet, and a little fuzzy ball for a tail. I think you are a bunny rabbit!" The rabbit, much relieved to discover his identity, proceeded to return the favor to the snake.

After feeling the snake's body for a few minutes he asserted, "You're scaly and slimy, you've got little beady eyes, you squirm and slither, and you've got a forked tongue. I think you're a lawyer!"

A JUDGE, BORED AND FRUSTRATED BY A lawyer's tedious arguments, had made numerous rulings to speed the trial along. The attorney had bristled at the judge's orders and tempers grew hot.

Finally, after another round of repetitious arguments, the judge pointed to his ear and said, "Counselor, you should be aware that, at this point, everything you say just goes in one ear and out the other."

"Your Honor, that goes without saying," replied the attorney. "What is there to prevent it?"

A lawyer and an engineer were fishing in the Caribbean when they got to talking. The lawyer mentioned, "I'm here because my house burned down and everything I owned was destroyed by the fire. The insurance company paid for everything."

"That's quite a coincidence," remarked the engineer. "I'm here because my house and all my belongings were destroyed by a flood. My insurance company, too, paid for everything."

There was a brief pause, and then the puzzled lawyer asked, "How do you start a flood?"

A CITY JUDGE WAS HEARING A DRUNK-driving case. The defendant, who had both a record and a reputation for driving under the influence, demanded a jury trial. It was nearly four o'clock, and knowing that putting together a jury would take time, the judge called a recess and went out to the hall looking to impanel anyone available.

He found a dozen lawyers in the main lobby, and told them that they were now a jury. The lawyers thought this would be a novel experience, and willingly followed the judge back to the courtroom.

Since it was clear that the defendant was guilty, the trial was over in about ten minutes. The jury went into the jury room and the judge started to pack up his things, sure of a quick decision. But after three hours, there was still no word on a verdict. The judge, now out of patience, sent the bailiff in the jury room to see what the hold-up was.

When the bailiff returned, the judge asked, "Well, have they got a verdict yet?"

The bailiff shook his head and said, "Verdict? Hell, they're still doing the nominating speeches for the foreman's position!"

A stingy old lawyer, diagnosed with a terminal illness, was determined to prove wrong the saying, "You can't take it with you."

After much thought and consideration, the old ambulance chaser finally figured out how to take at least some of his money with him when he died. He instructed his wife to go to the bank and withdraw enough money to fill two pillowcases. He then directed her to take the bags of money to the attic and leave them directly over his bed. His plan: When he passed away, he would reach out and grab the bags on his way to heaven.

Several weeks after the funeral, the deceased lawyer's wife came upon the two forgotten pillowcases while cleaning the attic. "Oh, that darned old fool," she exclaimed. "I knew he should have told me to put the money in the basement."

WHY DO LAWYERS DISPLAY A COPY OF their bar association cards on their dashboards?

So they can park in handicapped zones; it's proof of a moral disability.

You seem to have more than the average share of intelligence for a man of your background," sneered the lawyer at a witness on the stand.

"If I weren't under oath, I'd return the compliment," replied the witness.

THE MINUTE YOU READ SOMETHING YOU don't understand, you can be almost sure it was drawn up by a lawyer.

—Will Rogers

A paralegal, an associate, and a partner of a prestigious law firm were walking through a city park when they found an antique oil lamp. The paralegal gave it a rub, and out came a genie in a puff of smoke.

"Well, this is unusual," the genie said. "I only

grant three wishes, so I'll give each of you just one."

"Me first! Me first!" said the associate. "I want to be in the Bahamas, driving a speedboat with a handsome man."

Poof! She was gone.

"Me next! Me next!" said the paralegal. "I want to be in Hawaii, relaxing on the beach with a professional hula dancer on one side and a Mai Tai on the other."

Poof! He was gone.

"You're next," the genie said to the partner.

The partner smiled. "I want those two back in the office after lunch."

A SMALL-TOWN PROSECUTING ATTORNEY called his first witness, a grandmotherly woman, to the stand. He approached her and asked, "Mrs. Jones, do you know me?"

"Why, yes I do, Mr. Williams," she responded. "I've known you since you were a young boy. And frankly, you've been a big disappointment to me. You lie, you cheat on your wife, you manipulate people and talk about them behind their backs. You think you're a rising big-shot when you haven't the brains to realize you will never amount to anything more than a two-bit paper pusher."

The lawyer was stunned. Regaining his composure, he pointed across the room and asked, "Mrs. Jones, do you know the defense attorney?"

"Why, yes, I know him, too," she replied. "I used to baby-sit him, as a matter of fact. And he, too, has been a real disappointment to me. He's lazy, bigoted, and he has a drinking problem. The man can't build a decent relationship with anyone, and his law practice is one of the shoddiest in the state."

At this point, the judge rapped his gavel and ordered the courtroom to silence. He called both counselors to the bench. In a very quiet, menacing voice he ordered, "If either of you asks her if she knows me, you'll be jailed for contempt!"

A lawyer died and went to heaven, where he appeared before God. "A lawyer, eh?" said God. "We've never had a lawyer in heaven before. Argue a point of the law for my edification."

The lawyer went into a panic and said, "Oh, God, I can't think of an argument worthy of your notice. But I'll tell you what—you argue a point of the law and I'll refute you."

THE PROMINENT MIDDLE-AGED ATTORNEY was walking alone in the woods when he heard a booming voice from above declare, "You are going to live to be one hundred."

That must be God speaking, the attorney thought. Figuring that now he had ample time to make amends in order to enter heaven, the attorney began doing good deeds that very evening. But the next day, just as he was leaving the homeless shelter where he had volunteered an hour of his time, he was hit by a bus and killed.

When the attorney came face to face with

God, he started to protest. "You promised me I was going to live to be one hundred. Instead, the very first day I did a good deed, a bus hits me and here I am. What's the deal?"

"I didn't recognize you," God replied.

ANONYMOUSLY WRITTEN ON A LAW
school wall:
  "In law school, time is meaningless; but in
time, law school is meaningless."

A lawyer, driving by a Texas ranch, hit
and killed a calf crossing the road. He
found the owner of the ranch, explained
what happened, and asked what the animal was
worth.
  "Oh, about $200 today," said the rancher.
"But in six years it would have been worth
$900. So, $900 is really what I'm out."
  The lawyer promptly wrote out a check and
handed it to the rancher.
  "Here is your check for $900," he said. "It's
post-dated six years from today."

AN ATTORNEY, ADDRESSING THE JURY,
spoke of his client on trial for killing his parents: "Dear ladies and gentleman, please take
mercy and release this poor orphan."

I USED TO BE A LAWYER, BUT NOW I'M A reformed character.

—Woodrow Wilson

The senior lawyer wanted to teach the junior lawyer how to hire a new secretary, so he asked the young lad to sit in on two interviews that morning.

The first female candidate nervously walked into the law firm's conference room. The senior lawyer invited her to sit down, and then said, "I just have one question to ask you. How much is two and two?"

The first interviewee paused, thought carefully, and then queried: "Now when you say two and two, do you mean two plus two, two times two, or twenty-two?"

Escorting the young woman out the door, the senior attorney abruptly responded, "Thanks. That's all. I'll get back to you."

A short time later, the next candidate arrived. Again, the senior attorney sat her down, and then asked the same question: "How much is two and two?"

THE BEST LAWYER JOKES EVER

This young woman answered, without hesitation, "Four."

The senior lawyer promptly dismissed the second interviewee as well, saying, "Thanks. That's all. I'll get back to you."

At this point, the junior lawyer turned to the senior lawyer. "Wow! That was amazing," he exclaimed. "You asked one simple question. The first woman gave you such a thoughtful, inquisitive response; then again, the second woman was so direct and to the point. Tell me, counselor, which of the two women have you decided to hire as your new secretary?"

"Ain't it obvious?" smirked the senior lawyer. "The one with the nicer legs!"

TWO FRIENDS, SUE AND STEVE, MET ON the street after not having seen each other for some time. Sue was surprised to see Steve using crutches.

"Hello!" said Sue. "What's the matter with you?"

"Car accident," replied Steve.

"When did it happen?"

"Oh, about six weeks ago."

"And you still have to use crutches?"

"Well," said Steve, "my doctor says I could get along without them, but my lawyer says I can't."

Taking his seat in his chambers, the small-town judge faced the opposing lawyers.

"I have been presented, by both of you, with a bribe," the judge began. Both lawyers squirmed uncomfortably. "You, Attorney Leoni, gave me $15,000. And you, Attorney Campos, gave me $10,000."

The judge reached into his pocket and pulled out a check, which he handed to Leoni. "Now then, I'm returning $5,000, and we are going to decide this case solely on its merits."

TWO LAWYERS, JON AND BOB, HEADED out for their usual nine holes of golf. Jon bet Bob $50 that he would win the game. Bob,

feeling competitive, was willing to take
the bet.

They both played a great game. Bob was
ahead by one stroke after the eighth hole, but
on the ninth he cut his ball into the rough.

"C'mon, help me find my ball," he pleaded
with Jon. "Look over there."

After searching for a few minutes, they still
hadn't found the ball. Remembering that a lost
ball carries a four-point penalty, Bob pulled
another one from his pocket and tossed it to
the ground. "I've found my ball!" he announced.

Jon glared at him. "After all the years we've
been partners and playing together, I can't
believe you'd cheat me out of a lousy fifty
bucks!"

"What do you mean, cheat? I found my ball
sitting right there!"

"And you're a liar, too!" Jon cried. "I'll have
you know I've been *standing* on your ball for
the last five minutes!"

A lawyer entered a bank as a robber was making his getaway. Noticing the customers with their faces buried in the floor and the tellers with their hands in the air, the lawyer asked what had happened.

As the bank manager dialed the police department he shouted, "That man just walked out of here with $1 million!"

"One million dollars!" the lawyer answered in shock. "Why didn't you say something? I would have given him my card!"

LAW SCHOOLS HAVE BEEN DESCRIBED AS "a place for the accumulation of learning"— first-year students bring some in, third-year students bring some out, and, as a result, knowledge accumulates.

Gary went to his lawyer and said, "I would like to make a will, but I don't know exactly how to go about it."

"Don't worry," his lawyer replied, "leave it all to me."

Gary began to get upset. "Well, I knew you were going to take the biggest slice, but I'd like to leave a little to my children, too!"

IN A TERRIBLE ACCIDENT AT A RAILROAD crossing, a train smashed into a car and pushed it nearly 400 yards down the track. Though no one was killed, the driver took the railroad to court.

At the trial, the engineer insisted that he had given the driver ample warning by waving his lantern back and forth for nearly a minute. He even stood and convincingly demonstrated how he'd done it. The court believed his story, and the suit was dismissed.

"Congratulations," the lawyer said to the engineer when it was over. "You did superbly under cross-examination."

"Thanks," he said, "but he sure had me worried."

"How's that?" the lawyer asked.

"I was afraid he was going to ask if the lantern was lit!"

Attorney Jacobson decided to get away from the office and go skiing for a week. On his second day there, just a few moments after he had headed down the slope, he heard a rumbling from above. Several seconds later a huge mass of snow came rushing towards him. Luckily, Jacobson was right by a cave, and he jumped in before the snow hit. He was even luckier to find some matches on him and some dry wood in the cave. Within a few minutes, Jacobson was able to start a fire.

Back at the resort, people realized that the lawyer had not returned, and a rescue team was sent out in search of him. After a few hours, the team saw smoke coming from within the snow. One rescuer dug down and poked his head inside. "Are you there, Mr. Jacobson? This is the Red Cross."

Bristling, the lawyer called back, "Get lost! I gave at the office!"

HAVE YOU HEARD ABOUT THE LAWYERS' word processor?

No matter what font you select, everything comes out in fine print.

The lawyer was talking to his client, who was just convicted of murder.

"I have some good news, and some bad news," the lawyer said. "The bad news is that you're getting the electric chair."

His client said, "That's terrible! Well, what's the good news?"

"I got the voltage lowered."

THE NEW YORK TIMES, AMONG OTHER papers, recently published a new Hubble Space Telescope photograph of distant galaxies colliding.

Of course, astronomers have had pictures of colliding galaxies for quite some time now, but with the vastly improved resolution provided by the Hubble, you can actually see the lawyers rushing to the scene.

And God said: "Let there be Satan, so people don't blame everything on me. And let there be lawyers, so people don't blame everything on Satan."

—George Burns

A LAWYER, DEFENDING A MAN ACCUSED of burglary, tried this creative defense: "My client merely inserted his arm into the window and removed a few trifling articles. His arm is not himself, and I fail to see how you can punish the whole individual for an offense committed by his limb."

"Well put," the judge replied. "Using your logic, I sentence the defendant's arm to one year's imprisonment. He can accompany it or not, as he chooses."

The defendant smiled. With his lawyer's assistance, he detached his artificial limb, laid it on the bench, and walked out.

How to be a good lawyer:
    1) When the law is against you, argue the facts.

2) When the facts are against you, argue the law.

3) When both are against you, call the other lawyers names.

A RABBI, A HINDU, AND A LAWYER WERE driving late at night in the country when their car broke down. They set out to find help and came across a farmhouse. When they knocked at the door, the farmer explained that he had only two beds, and one of the three had to sleep in the barn with the animals. The three quickly agreed. The Rabbi generously said he would sleep in the barn and let the other two have the beds.

Ten minutes after the Rabbi left, there was a knock on the bedroom door. The Rabbi entered exclaiming, "I'm sorry, but I can't sleep in the barn; there is a pig in there. It's against my religion to sleep in the same room with a pig!" The Hindu said that *he* would sleep in the barn, as he had no religious issue with pigs.

However, about five minutes later, the Hindu burst through the bedroom door saying, "There's a *cow* in the barn! I can't sleep in the same room as a cow! It's against my religion!" The lawyer, anxious to get to sleep, said he'd go to the barn, as he had no problem sleeping with either animal.

In two minutes, the bedroom door burst open and the pig and the cow entered.

A pickpocket was up in court for a series of petty crimes. The judge delivered his sentence: "Mr. Banks, you are hereby fined $100."

The lawyer stood up and said, "Thank you, Your Honor. Unfortunately my client only has $75 on him at this time, but if you'd allow him a few minutes in the crowd . . ."

AT TWO IN THE MORNING, THE PHONE rang at the governor's mansion. An aide found himself talking to a local attorney, who insisted that he must speak with the governor immediately. Despite pleas to postpone his call until morning, the attorney insisted that the call was a matter of utmost urgency, and he could not wait. The aide reluctantly decided to wake the governor.

"What is it?" grumbled the governor as he picked up the phone.

"Judge Cassidy just died," announced the attorney, "and I want to take his place."

The governor shot back, "It's okay with me if it's okay with the undertaker."

WHAT DO YOU CALL A LAWYER WITH AN
I.Q. of 50?
  Your Honor.

A lawyer and this beautiful, perfect woman, a "ten" if you will, got into an elevator together. Miss Ten pushed one of the penthouse floors and looked demurely at the lawyer. "You know what I would like to do with you right now?" she asked.

The lawyer said, "What? And, by the way, my billing rate is $500 an hour, so it is in your pecuniary interest to say whatever you have to say in the most succinct terms. Where may I send the bill?"

Miss Ten said, breathlessly, "Well, what I would like to do is take you to my little *pied a terre*, and take off all your clothes. I'd rub your back in my 500-gallon bubble bath tub, then rub oil over every part of your body. As the *piece de resistance*, I'd make wild, passionate love to you." She rubbed up next to the lawyer. "Do you think that you can fit *that* into your busy schedule?"

The lawyer looked at Miss Ten, and then checked his watch to get the precise amount of time this consultation consumed. He looked up and asked, "Okay, I see what is in it for you, but what's in it for me?"

"YOUR HONOR," A DEFENSE ATTORNEY began, "I have a series of witnesses that can testify that Mr. Johnson was nowhere near the scene of the crime when it occurred."

The judge looked at the defense table and said, "This is the third time you've been in this courtroom this week, and I'm getting sick of hearing your lies."

The defendant stood up with a confused expression. "With all due respect, Your Honor, you must be mistaken. I've never been here in my life."

Waving his finger, the judge replied, "I was referring to your lawyer."

Two attorneys, Tavolott and Regan, took a long safari vacation in the African Bush. While walking one day they stopped to rest, removing their packs and leaning their rifles against a tree. They were startled when a large, hungry-looking lion emerged from the jungle and began eyeing them with anticipation. It was clear that the attorneys' rifles were too far away to do them any good.

Tavolott began to remove his shoes. Regan looked at him quizzically. "Why are you doing that?"

"I can run faster without them," Tavolott answered.

Regan snickered. "I don't care how fast you can run. You'll never out-race that lion."

"I don't have to out-race that lion," Tavolott replied. "I just have to out-race you."

Q: HOW MANY LAWYERS DOES IT TAKE to change a light bulb?

A: Whereas the party of the first part, also known as "Lawyer," and the party of the second part, also known as "Light Bulb," do hereby and forthwith agree to a transaction wherein the party of the second part (Light Bulb) shall be removed from the current position as a result of failure to perform previously agreed upon duties, i.e., the lighting, elucidation, and otherwise illumination of the area ranging from the front (north) door, through the entryway, terminating at an area just inside the primary living area, demarcated by the beginning of the carpet, any spillover illumination being at the option of the party of the second part (Light Bulb) and not required by the aforementioned agreement between the parties.

The aforementioned removal transaction shall include, but not be limited to, the following steps: 1) The party of the first part (Lawyer) shall, with or without elevation at his option, by means of a chair, stepstool, ladder or any other means of elevation, grasp the party of the second part (Light Bulb) and rotate the party of the second part (Light Bulb) in a counter-clockwise direction, this point being non-negotiable.

2) Upon reaching a point where the party of the second part (Light Bulb) becomes separated from the party of the third part ("Receptacle"), the party of the first part (Lawyer) shall have the option of disposing of the party of the second part (Light Bulb) in a manner consistent with all applicable state, local and federal statutes.

3) Once separation and disposal have been achieved, the party of the first part (Lawyer) shall have the option of beginning installation of the party of the fourth part ("New Light Bulb"). This installation shall occur in a manner consistent with the reverse of the procedures described in step one of this self-same document, being careful to note that the rotation should occur in a clockwise direction, this point also being non-negotiable. NOTE: The above described steps may be performed, at

the option of the party of the first part (Lawyer), by any or all persons authorized by him, the objective being to produce the most possible revenue for the party of the fifth part, also known as "Partnership."

IT IS BETTER TO BE A MOUSE IN A CAT'S mouth than a man in a lawyer's hands.
—Spanish Proverb

Two lawyers, Smith and Frankel, met for a drink one evening after work.

Smith says, "You'll never believe what happened to me! I ran into an angel, who told me he was sent down from heaven to compile a list of the dishonest lawyers on earth. Six months later he dragged himself back to heaven, exhausted. 'Believe me,' he told God, 'It would be easier if I just made a list of all of the honest lawyers on earth. In fact, I think I could do that in a weekend.' God agreed, and come Monday morning the angel turned in his list. God said, 'That's terrific. Now I think you should send all the lawyers on this list a note of congratulations.'"

Smith paused and took a sip of his gin and tonic. Then he continued. "There was a post-script to the angel's note. You know what it was?"

Harry shook his head, incredulous. "No."

"Aha! So you didn't get a note, either!"

MURRAY MUFFSTEIN'S WIFE, PHYLLIS, died quite suddenly. As the mourners approached the grave, they were appalled to see that the tombstone read, "Here lies Phyllis, wife of Murray Muffstein, L.L.D., Wills, Divorce, Malpractice."

Suddenly, Murray burst into tears. His brother exclaimed, "For land's sake, you *should* cry, pulling a stunt like this!"

Through his tears, Murray croaked, "You don't understand. They left out the phone number!"

WHILE WALKING PAST THE CITY COURTS one afternoon, a man spotted his friend sitting on the steps outside, sobbing loudly with his head buried in his hands.

"What's the matter?" he asked his friend. "Did your lawyer give you bad advice?"

"No, it's worse than that," his friend replied between sobs. "He sold it to me."

A man walked into a bar and saw a beautiful, well-dressed woman sitting on a barstool. He went up to her and said in a low voice, "Hi there, how's it going tonight?"

She turned to him, looked him straight in the eyes and replied, "I'll screw anybody at any time, anywhere—your place or my place, it doesn't matter to me."

The man raised his eyebrows and said, "No kidding! What law firm do you work for?"

THERE ARE TWO KINDS OF LAWYERS— those who know the law and those who know the judge.

LAWYER: DO YOU WISH TO CHALLENGE any of the jury members?

Defendant: Well, I think I could lick that little guy on the end!

The old man was critically ill. Sensing that he was at death's door, he called his attorney.

"I want to become a lawyer. How much is it for that express degree you told me about?"

"It's $50,000," his attorney said, "But why? You'll be dead soon, why do you want to become a lawyer?"

"That's my business! Just get me the course!"

Four days later, the old man got his law degree. His lawyer was at his bedside making sure his bill would be paid.

Suddenly the old man was racked with fits of coughing and it was clear that the end was near. Curious, the lawyer leaned over and said, "Please, before it's too late, tell me why you wanted to get a law degree so badly before you died?"

The old man replied in a faint whisper, as he breathed his last breath, "One less lawyer!"

AT THE HEIGHT OF A POLITICAL corruption trial, the prosecuting attorney attacked a witness.

"Isn't it true," he bellowed, "that you accepted $5,000 to compromise this case?"

The witness stared out the window, as though he hadn't heard the question.

"Isn't it true that you accepted $5,000 to compromise this case?" the lawyer repeated. The witness still did not respond.

Finally, the judge leaned over and said, "Sir, please answer the question."

"Oh," the startled witness said, "I thought he was talking to you."

How is it you can't get a lawyer to defend you?" the judge asked the prisoner.

"Well, Yer Honor, it's like this. As soon as those lawyers found out I didn't steal the money, they wouldn't have anything to do with me."

A BIG-CITY LAWYER WENT DUCK HUNTING in rural Arizona. He shot and dropped a bird, but it fell into a farmer's field on the other side of a fence. As the lawyer climbed over the fence, an elderly farmer drove up on his tractor and asked what he was doing.

"I shot a duck and it fell into this field," the litigator responded. "Now I'm going to retrieve it."

The old farmer shook his head. "This is my property and you are not coming over here."

"I am one of the best trial attorneys in the country, and if you don't let me get that duck I'll sue you and take everything you own."

The old farmer simply smiled. "Apparently, you don't know how we do things in Arizona. We settle small disagreements like this with the Arizona Three Kick Rule."

"What is the Arizona Three Kick Rule?"

"Well, first I kick you three times and then you kick me three times, and so on, back and forth, until someone gives up," the farmer stated. The attorney quickly thought about the proposed contest and decided that he could easily take the old codger. He agreed to abide by the local custom.

The old farmer slowly climbed down from the tractor and walked up to the city fellow. His first kick planted the toe of his heavy work boot into the lawyer's groin and dropped him to his knees. His second kick nearly wiped the man's nose off his face. The barrister was flat on his belly when the farmer's third kick to a kidney nearly caused him to give up.

The lawyer summoned every bit of his will and managed to get to his feet and said, "Okay, you old goat! Now, it's my turn!"

The old farmer grinned and said, "Naw, I give up. You can have the duck."

An Associate Justice of the Supreme Court was sitting by a river when a Traveler approached and said:

"I wish to cross. Will it be lawful to use this boat?"

"It will," was the reply. "It is my boat."

The Traveler thanked him, and pushing the

boat into the water embarked and rowed away. But the boat sank and he was drowned.

"Heartless man!" said an Indignant Spectator. "Why did you not tell him that your boat had a hole in it?"

"The matter of the boat's condition," said the great jurist, "was not brought before me."
—Ambrose Bierce, *Fantastic Fables*, 1899

AFTER HIS MOTION TO SUPPRESS evidence was denied by the court, the angered attorney spoke up. "Your Honor," he said, "what would you do if I called you a stupid, degenerate, old fool?"

The judge, now also angered, revered, "I would hold you in contempt of court and seek to have you suspended from practicing before this court again!"

"What if I only thought it?" asked the attorney.

"Well, in that case, there is nothing I could do. You have the right to think whatever you want."

"Oh, I see. Then, if it pleases the court," the attorney announced, "let the record reflect that I *think* you're a stupid, degenerate, old fool!"

A pedestrian was standing on the sidewalk when he saw a funeral procession. The procession had two hearses followed by a man walking a dog. Directly behind the man was a single-file line of at least two hundred people. Curious, the pedestrian approached the man walking the dog and asked what was going on. The man with the dog explained that in the first hearse was his ex-wife's lawyer. The dog had bitten the lawyer and two days later the man had died.

The pedestrian then asked about the second hearse, whereupon the man with the dog explained that he was the lawyer who had represented the man's former business partner in a long and vicious business break-up. The other lawyer, too, had been bitten by the dog, and had died two days later. The pedestrian pondered this information for a moment, then whispered in the dog owner's ear, "Say, would you mind if I borrowed your dog for a while?"

Without missing a step, the dog owner replied, "It's okay by me, fella, but you're gonna have to wait your turn in line like everyone else."

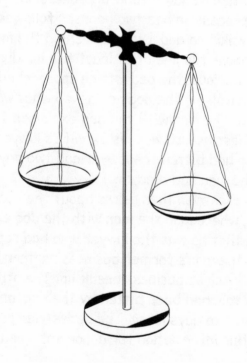

CHANGING LAWYERS IS LIKE MOVING TO a different deck chair on the Titanic.

A lawyer, who was talking to his son about entering college, was miffed. "Now you've got it into your head that you want to be a doctor instead of a lawyer?" he asked.

"Well, Dad," answered his son, "did you ever hear anybody get up in a crowd and frantically shout, 'Is there a lawyer in the house?'"

PHIL WAS CALLED AS A WITNESS IN A criminal case in which the defendant, acting as his own counsel, was frequently reprimanded by the judge for badgering the witness. Finally, this self-attorney closed with one last question: "You really don't like the defendant, do you?"

The witness sat back in his chair for a moment, then leaned into the microphone. "I really don't know anything about the defendant," he said, "but I've taken a strong dislike to his attorney."

During cross-examination, a slightly unsure witness to a car crash kept saying things like, "I think the light was yellow" or "I think it was still raining."

The cross-examining lawyer interrupted, saying derisively, "We don't care what you *think*. What do you *know*?"

The harried witness paused for a moment and then replied, "Then I may as well leave the witness stand. Since I'm not a lawyer, I can't talk without thinking."

IN THE LAW, THE ONLY THING CERTAIN is the expense.

—Samuel Butler

A doctor, a lawyer, a little boy, and a priest were out for a Sunday afternoon flight on a small private plane. The plane suddenly developed engine trouble. In spite of the pilot's best efforts, the plane started to go down. The pilot grabbed a parachute and yelled to the passengers that they had better jump, too. He opened up the hatch and bailed out.

Unfortunately, there were only three parachutes remaining. The doctor grabbed one, saying, "I'm a doctor. I save lives, so I must live." He jumped out of the plane.

The lawyer then grabbed the next one, saying, "I'm a lawyer and lawyers are the smartest people in the world. I deserve to live." He, too, jumped out of the plane.

The priest looked at the little boy and said, "My son, I've lived a long and full life. You are young and have many years ahead of you. Please, take the last parachute and live in peace."

The little boy handed the parachute back to the priest. "Not to worry, Father. The 'smartest man in the world' just took off with my backpack."

"YOU ARE A CHEAT!" SHOUTED THE attorney to his opponent.

"And you're a liar!" bellowed the opposition.

Banging his gavel sharply, the judge interrupted: "All right, all right. Now that both attorneys have been identified, let's get on with this case."

While questioning a panel for prospective jury members, the lawyer began to fire off questions in the manner of an intimidating showman. As he was finishing up his questioning, he asked, "Do any of you here today dislike lawyers?"

Before the pause became too long, the judge announced, "I do."

CRAIG WENT TO HIS LAWYER'S FUNERAL, and was surprised by the tremendous turnout for one man. He whispered to the woman sitting next to him, "This is amazing. Who are all these people? Family? Friends?"

The woman leaned over and whispered back, "We're all clients."

"And you *all* came to pay your respects? How touching."

"No." She shook her head. "We came to make sure he was dead."

Q: How many lawyers does it take to change a light bulb?

A: None. He'll have the janitor do it. But you'll get the following bill:

Item Charge (and what it really means)

• Lawyer's time (1 hr. minimum): $400 (you sucker)

• Connectivity charge: $100 (he called janitor)

• Staff charges: $250 (secretary prepared bill)

• Research fees: $422 (BMW payment due)

• Consulting fees: $431 (Sr. Partner's BMW payment)

• Specialized equipment: $122 (bought bulb)

• Delivery expenses: $34 (had messenger deliver bulb)

• Rule 453.957(B)(1) charge: $394 (second partner's Volvo payment)

THREE PARAMEDICS WERE BOASTING about improvements in their respective ambulance team's response times.

"Since we installed our new satellite navigation system," bragged the first paramedic, "we've cut our emergency response time by 10 percent."

The other paramedics nodded in approval. "Not bad," the second paramedic commented. "But by using a model of traffic patterns, we've cut our average ERT by 30 percent."

Again, the other team members gave their congratulations, until the third paramedic said, "That's nothing! Since our ambulance driver passed the bar exam, we've cut our emergency response time in half!"

I BROKE A MIRROR IN MY HOUSE. I'M supposed to get seven years of bad luck, but my lawyer thinks he can get me five.

A lawyer, discussing trial strategy with his partner, said, "When I address the jury, I'll plead for clemency."

"Nothing doing!" shouted his partner. "Let Clemency get his own lawyer."

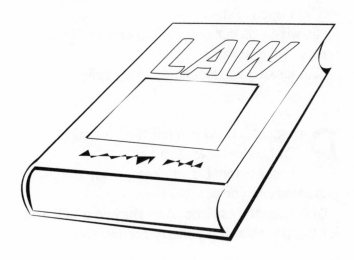

A LAWYER, ON HIS DEATHBED, CALLED OUT to his wife to bring in the Bible.

Being a religious woman, she thought this was a wonderful idea. She ran and brought it to him, preparing to read him his favorite verse. Instead, he snatched it from her and began to quickly scan the pages, his eyes darting left and right.

His wife was curious. "What are you doing, honey?" she asked.

"I'm looking for loopholes," he replied.

Prosecutor: Did you kill the victim?
Defendant: No, I did not.
Prosecutor: Do you know what the penalties are for perjury?
Defendant: Yes, I do. And they're a hell of a lot better than the penalty for murder.

IN THE HALLS OF JUSTICE, THE ONLY justice is in the halls.

—Lenny Bruce

A MEXICAN BANDIT MADE A SPECIALTY of crossing the Rio Grande and robbing banks in Texas. A reward was finally offered for his capture, and an enterprising Texas Ranger decided to track him down.

After a lengthy search, he traced the bandit to his favorite cantina. The ranger snuck up behind him, put his trusty six-shooter to the bandit's head, and said, "You're under arrest. Tell me where you hid the loot or I'll blow your brains out."

But the bandit didn't speak English, and the ranger didn't speak Spanish. Fortunately, a bilingual lawyer was in the saloon and translated the ranger's message. The terrified bandit blurted out, in Spanish, that the loot was buried under the oak tree in back of the cantina.

"What did he say?" demanded the ranger.

The lawyer answered, "He said, 'Get lost, you turkey. You wouldn't dare shoot me.'"

One afternoon, a barber gave a haircut to a priest. The priest tried to pay for the haircut, but the barber refused, saying, "You do God's work." The next morning, the barber found a dozen Bibles at the door to his shop.

A policeman came to the barber for a haircut, and again the barber refused payment, saying, "You protect the public." The next morning the barber found a dozen donuts at the door to his shop.

A lawyer came to the barber for a haircut, and the barber refused payment for a third time. "You serve the justice system," he said. The next morning, the barber found a dozen lawyers waiting for a free haircut.

TWO SMART, ATTRACTIVE, WELL-educated young law graduates, Sally and Edith, were competing for a prestigious job. As part of the job interview, each candidate was asked why she wanted the position.

Edith answered that she wanted to work for a firm with a reputation for being concerned with truth and justice. When it was her turn, Sally simply opened her purse, took out a rather thin wallet, and laid it on the senior partner's desk. "I want to fatten this up as fast as possible," she said.

Sally got the job.

A defendant was asked if he wanted a bench trial or a jury trial. "Jury trial," he replied.

"Do you understand the difference?" asked the judge.

"Sure," replied the defendant, "That's where twelve ignorant people decide my fate instead of one."

CHILDREN WHO NEVER COME WHEN they are called will grow up to be doctors.

Children who come before they are called will grow up to be lawyers.

A man was on trial for a murder in a small town. There was strong evidence indicating guilt; however, there was no corpse. In the defense's closing statement the lawyer, knowing that his client will most likely be convicted, resorted to a clever trick.

"Ladies and gentleman of the jury, I have a surprise for you all," the lawyer said as he looked at his watch. "Within one minute, the person presumed dead in this case will walk into this courtroom." He looked toward the courtroom door. The jury, somewhat stunned, all looked on eagerly.

A minute passed. Nothing happened.

The lawyer finally continued. "Actually, ladies and gentleman, I made up the following statement. But you all looked on with anticipation. I, therefore, put it to you that there is reasonable doubt in this case as to whether anyone was killed. I must insist that you return a verdict of not guilty."

The jury, clearly confused, retired to deliberate. A few minutes later, the jury returned and the foreman pronounced a verdict of guilty.

"But how?" inquired the incredulous lawyer.

"You must have had some doubt. I saw all of you stare at the door."

"Oh, we did look," responded the foreman. "But your client didn't."

AN ACCOUNTANT AND A LAWYER BUMPED into each other in the elevator one evening.

The accountant turned to the lawyer and commented, "Nice weather we're having, isn't it?"

As the attorney was about to reply, the accountant gasped and held up his hand. "Wait," he said, "don't answer that. I can't afford the fee for your opinion!"

A successful lawyer parked his brand-new Jag XK-8 in front of the office, ready to show it off to his colleagues. As he got out, a truck came too close to the curb, and completely tore off the driver's door of the Jag.

The attorney immediately grabbed his cell phone and dialed 911. It wasn't more than five minutes before a policeman pulled up. Before the cop had a chance to ask any questions, the lawyer started screaming hysterically. His Jag was now completely ruined and would never be the same again.

After the lawyer finally wound down from his rant, the cop shook his head in disgust. "I can't believe how materialistic you lawyers are," he said. "You're so focused on your possessions that you don't notice anything else?"

"How can you say such a thing?" asked the lawyer.

"Didn't you know that your left arm is missing from the elbow down?" replied the cop in disbelief. "It must have been torn off when the truck hit you!"

"My God!" screamed the lawyer. "Where's my Rolex?"

ARGUING WITH A LAWYER IS LIKE MUD wrestling with a pig. After a while, you realize that the pig is at home in the mud.

B arney was sent to hell for his sins. As he was being taken to his place of eternal torment, he saw a lawyer making love to a beautiful woman.

"What a rip-off," Barney muttered. "I have to roast for all eternity, and that lawyer gets to spend it with a beautiful woman."

Jabbing the man with his pitchfork, the escorting Satan snarled, "Who are you to question that woman's punishment?"

BETWEEN GRAND THEFT AND A LEGAL FEE,
    There only stands a law degree.

A ttorney Millman had just successfully defended a major crime lord from charges of drug dealing, racketeering, murder, kidnapping, and selling arms.

As he left the courtroom, an indignant old woman grabbed him by the arm. "Young man, I am appalled! Where are your Christian scruples? I do believe you would defend Satan himself!"

"That depends," Attorney Millman calmly replied. "What has your kid done?"

AN AIRLINER WAS HAVING ENGINE trouble, and the pilot instructed the cabin crew to have the passengers take their seats and prepare for an emergency landing. A few minutes later, the pilot asked the flight attendants if everyone was buckled in and ready.

"All set back here, Captain," came the reply, "except one lawyer who is still passing out business cards."

Experts are people who know a great deal about very little. They go along learning more and more about less and less until they know practically everything about nothing.

Lawyers, on the other hand, are people who know very little about many things. They keep learning less and less about more and more until they know practically nothing about everything.

Judges are people who start out knowing everything about everything, but end up knowing nothing about anything because of their constant association with experts and lawyers.

A GRADE SCHOOL TEACHER WAS ASKING students what their parents did for a living. "Tim, you go first," she said. "What does your mother do all day?"

Tim stood up and proudly said, "She's a doctor."

"That's wonderful. How about you, Amy?"

Amy shyly stood up, scuffled her feet, and said, "My father is a mailman."

"Thank you, Amy," said the teacher. "What about your father, Billy?"

Billy proudly stood up and announced, "My daddy plays piano in a whorehouse."

The teacher was aghast and promptly changed the subject to geography. Later that day, she went to Billy's house and was greeted by his father. The teacher recounted what his son had said, and demanded an explanation.

"I'm actually an attorney," Billy's father replied. "But how do you explain a thing like that to a seven-year-old?"

At a meeting of the bar association, a famous attorney was boasting about his new glass eye. He claimed that it was so realistic that no one could tell which was the false one.

All of the lawyer's present nodded in astonished belief, while a layman present blurted out, "It's obvious that the left one is phony!"

The attorney, shocked that his secret was so easily discovered, asked the layman how he knew.

"Why, it's easy," he replied. "The fake one is the eye with a gleam of humanity."

A lawyer was on vacation in a small farming town. While walking through the streets on a quiet Sunday morning, he came upon a large crowd gathered by the side of the road. Going by instinct, the lawyer figured that there was some sort of auto collision. He was eager to get to the injured parties, but couldn't get near the car. Being a clever sort, he started shouting loudly, "Let me through! Let me through! I am the son of the victim."

The crowd made way for him. Lying in front of the car was a donkey.

HEAR ABOUT THE LADY LAWYER WHO dropped her briefs and became a solicitor?

A YOUNG BOY WALKED UP TO HIS FATHER and asked, "Dad, does a lawyer ever tell the truth?"

The father thought for a moment. "Yes, son. Sometimes a lawyer will do anything to win a case."

An American attorney had just finished a guest lecture at a law school in Italy. As he was walking out of the school, an Italian attorney approached him with his partner. "I thought your lecture was just wonderful. But I had to ask you a question: Is it true that a person can fall down on a sidewalk in your country and then sue the landowners for lots of money?"

Told that it was true, the lawyer turned to his partner and started speaking rapidly in Italian. When they stopped, the pleased American attorney asked if they wanted to go to America to practice law.

"No, no," the Italian attorney replied. "We want to go to America and fall down on sidewalks."

TWO PHYSICIANS BOARDED A FLIGHT OUT of Seattle. One sat in the window seat, the other sat in the middle seat. Just before takeoff, an attorney got on and took the aisle seat next to the two physicians.

The attorney kicked off his shoes, wiggled his toes and was settling in when the physician in the window seat said, "I think I'll get up and get a soda."

"Hey, don't get up," said the attorney. "I'll get it for you."

While he was gone, one of the physicians picked up the attorney's shoe and put a thumbtack in it. When he returned with the soda, the other physician said, "That looks good, I think I'll have one too."

Again, the attorney obligingly went to fetch it and while he was gone, the other physician picked up the other shoe and put a tack in it. The attorney returned and they all sat back and enjoyed the flight.

As the plane was landing, the attorney slipped his feet into his shoes and knew immediately what had happened.

"How long must this go on?" he asked. "This

fighting between our professions? This hatred? This animosity? This putting tacks in shoes and spitting in sodas?"

An owner of a bar was so sure that his bartender was the strongest man in the world that he offered $1,000 to anyone able to squeeze another drop of juice out of a lemon after his bartender squeezed all the juice out first. Many strong people had tried and failed.

One day a scrawny man came into the bar wearing thick glasses and a polyester suit. He squeaked, "I'd like to try the bet." After the laughter died down, the bartender grabbed a lemon and squeezed away. Then he handed the rind to the man, who, to everyone's amazement, squeezed another six drops into the glass.

Stunned, the bartender paid up, and then asked the man, "What do you do for a living? Are you a lumberjack? A weight lifter?"

"Nope," the man replied. "I'm an attorney for the IRS."

A PRIEST SETTLED INTO A CHAIR IN A lawyer's office. "Is it true," said the priest, "that your firm does not charge members of the clergy?"

"I'm afraid you're misinformed," stated the lawyer. "People in your profession can look forward to a reward in the next world, but we lawyers have to take ours in this one."

OLD LAWYERS NEVER DIE. THEY JUST establish law firms.

I, LUCIUS TITUS, HAVE WRITTEN THIS, my testament, without any lawyer, following my own natural reason rather than excessive and miserable diligence.
> —the will of a citizen of Rome

Zebrowski, a seasoned attorney, walked into a bar and sat down. The bartender went up to her and said, "What'll you have?"

She answered, "A scotch, please."

The bartender put the drink down in front of Zebrowski and stated, "That'll be $5."

Zebrowski frowned. "What are you talking about? I don't owe you anything for this."

Another attorney, sitting nearby, overheard the conversation. He said to the bartender, "You know, she's got you there. In the original offer, which constitutes a binding contract upon acceptance, there was no stipulation of remuneration."

The bartender was not impressed, but being a good sport said to Zebrowski, "Okay, okay, you beat me for a drink. But don't ever let me catch you in here again."

The very next day, Zebrowski walked into the bar. The bartender took one look at her and said, "What the hell are you doing in here? I can't believe you've got the audacity to come back!"

Zebrowski feigned shock. "What are you talking about? I've never been in this place in my life!"

The bartender apologetically replied, "Oh, I'm really sorry. This is uncanny. You must have a double."

"Thanks very much!" Zebrowski replied. "Make it a scotch."

SAM ENTERED A HOUSE OF ILL REPUTE IN San Francisco. The madam greeted him and asked his pleasure.

"Do you have a young lady with blonde hair and

blue eyes, named Mary?" Sam asked, adding, "She comes highly recommended."

"Why, yes we do," answered the madam. "Let me introduce you."

Sam meets Mary, and they retire to a convenient bedroom where the business was transacted. As Sam was getting dressed, he extracted his wallet from his pants and removed $500, which he lay on the table beside the bed.

Mary was very surprised, for he was paying far more than she usually got for this service, but she held her tongue.

"Boy, Mary!" Sam said. "You are the best I've ever had. Can I come back and see you again tomorrow?"

"Why, of course!" Mary smiled, thrilled at the prospect of a repeating such earnings again the next day.

Sam returned as promised, and again they retired to Mary's room. Upon completion, he took out $500 and placed the money on the bedside table.

Mary, who was becoming a little fond of Sam, said, "Uh, I probably shouldn't tell you this, but you're paying me too much. I usually make a $100, maybe $200 if it's really 'special,' but golly, $500?"

"That's okay, Mary," Sam said. "You're worth it! And I have one more day in town, so I'd like to come back one more time. That okay?"

"Why sure," Mary beamed. "I'll be looking for you."

Sam came the next day, and once it was over, as he was getting dressed, he took $1,000 from his wallet and laid it on the table.

Mary looked at the money, smiled, and said, "You are really something, y'know it? What line of work are you in, anyway?"

The man smiled brightly and said, "Oh, I'm an attorney, out here from North Carolina. An elderly client of mine, a Mrs. Cosgrove, died and I'm out here delivering a couple of thousand dollars inheritance to her niece."

A puzzled look crossed Mary's face. She paused, and then said, "Hmmm. That's funny—I think I've got an aunt named Cosgrove, and I think she lives in Fayetteville."

The attorney winked. "Gee, small world, isn't it?"

A n attorney observed a boy about nine years of age, diverting himself at play, whose eccentric appearance attracted his attention. "Come here my lad," said he. The boy accordingly came, and after chatting a bit, asked the attorney what case was to be tried next. "A case between the Pope and the devil," answered the attorney. "And which do you suppose will gain the action?"

"I don't know," said the boy, "I guess 'twill be a pretty tight squeeze; the Pope has the most money, but the devil has the most lawyers."

(The New-England Almanack for 1801)

A LAWYER'S CREED: A MAN IS INNOCENT until proven broke.

I f a lawyer and an IRS agent were both drowning, and you could only save one of them, would you go to lunch or read the paper?

A LAWYER APPROACHED THE JURY BOX
and began an eloquent plea for her client:
"Ladies and gentlemen of the jury, I want to
tell you about this man. There's so much to say
that is good. He never beat his mother. He
was always kind to little children. He never did
a dishonest thing in his life and he has always
lived by the golden rule. He is a model of
everything decent, forthright, and honest . . ."

Her client leaned over to a friend and said,
"How do like that woman? I pay her good
dough to defend me, and she's telling the jury
about some other guy."

A well-known evangelist of the last cen-
tury, Lorenzo Dow, arrived in a Kansas
town one very cold winter night. Looking
for heat, he went into the general store.
Around the stove were gathered the local
lawyers talking shop, not about to let a
stranger in to share the warmth.

When finally able to introduce himself, he
mentioned that he'd had a vision in a dream a

short time before. "Like Dante's immortal traveler, I was given a tour of hell."

"Well, Mr. Dow, what did you find there?" inquired one of his listeners.

"The same thing I find here," replied the preacher. "All the lawyers right in the hottest place."

They moved over and made room for him.

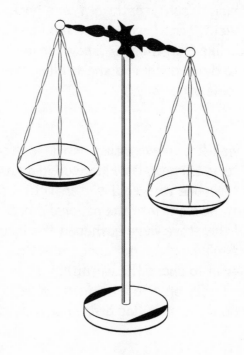

AN ENGINEER REPORTED TO THE GATES of hell and was let in. Pretty soon he became dissatisfied with the level of comfort there and started building improvements. After a short while, hell was equipped with air conditioning, flush toilets, and escalators, making the engineer a pretty popular guy.

One day God called Satan on the telephone and asked with a sneer, "So, how's it going down there in hell?"

"Hey, things are going great," Satan replied. "We've got air conditioning and flush toilets and escalators, and there's no telling what this engineer is going to come up with next."

"What?" God exclaimed. "You've got an engineer? That's a mistake. He should never had gone down there—send him back."

"No way!" Satan replied. "I like having an engineer on the staff, and I'm keeping him."

"Send him back up here or I'll sue!" God threatened.

Satan just laughed uproariously. "Ha! Yeah, right. And just where are *you* going to get a lawyer?"

P artners at a big law firm gathered for a picture at their annual dinner. All looked glum. The photographer tried several jokes to lighten the mood, but to no avail.

Finally, inspiration hit. He said, "Just say 'fees'!"